Here's all the great literature in this grade level of *Celebrate Reading!*

BOOK A

Once Upon a Hippo

Ways of Telling Stories

THREE UP A TREE
SAM
by James Marshall

There's a Hole in the Bucket

pictures by Nadine Bernard Westcott

Featured Poets

Beatrice Schenk de Regniers
Ed Young

JIMMY LEE DID IT
BY PAT CUMMINGS

BOOK B

The Big Blank Piece of Paper

Artists at Work

BOOK C

You Be the Bread and I'll Be the Cheese

Showing How We Care

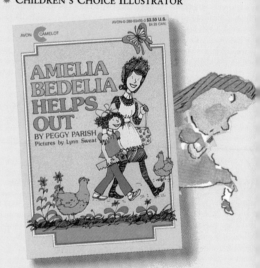

Featured Poets

Mary Ann Hoberman
Charlotte Pomerantz

BOOK D

Why Does Water Wiggle?

Learning About the World

Featured Poets

Jack Prelutsky
Lessie Jones Little

BOOK E
How to Talk to Bears
And Other Tips for Success

BOOK F
Bathtub Voyages
Tales of Adventure

Planet of the Grown-Ups
by Gus Gedatus
Illustrations by Marc Rosenthal

The Tub People
by Pam Conrad
Illustrations by Richard Egielski
* CHILDREN'S CHOICE
* ALA NOTABLE CHILDREN'S BOOK
* PARENTS' CHOICE

My Dog Is Lost!
by Ezra Jack Keats
and Pat Cherr
* CALDECOTT MEDAL ILLUSTRATOR

The Lost Lake
by Allen Say
* OUTSTANDING SCIENCE TRADE BOOK
* CALDECOTT MEDAL ILLUSTRATOR

Dinosaurs Travel:
A Guide for Families on the Go
from the book by
Laurie Krasny Brown
and Marc Brown
* TEACHERS' CHOICE AUTHOR
AND ILLUSTRATOR

Dinosaurs, Dragonflies, and
Diamonds: All About Natural
History Museums
by Gail Gibbons
* OUTSTANDING SCIENCE TRADE BOOK

Featured Poets

John Ciardi
Sioux Indian Songs

Celebrate Reading!
Trade Book Library

Frog and Toad Together
by Arnold Lobel
* NEWBERY MEDAL HONOR BOOK
* ALA NOTABLE CHILDREN'S BOOK
* SCHOOL LIBRARY JOURNAL BEST BOOK
* READING RAINBOW SELECTION
* LIBRARY OF CONGRESS
  CHILDREN'S BOOK

The Lady with the Alligator Purse
by Nadine Bernard Westcott
* CHILDREN'S CHOICE

Henry and Mudge in Puddle Trouble
by Cynthia Rylant
* GARDEN STATE CHILDREN'S
  BOOK AWARD

Tyrannosaurus Was a Beast
by Jack Prelutsky
* OUTSTANDING SCIENCE TRADE BOOK

A Chair for My Mother
by Vera Williams
* CALDECOTT MEDAL HONOR BOOK
* ALA NOTABLE CHILDREN'S BOOK
* READING RAINBOW SELECTION
* BOSTON GLOBE-HORN BOOK AWARD

Paul Bunyan
by Steven Kellogg
* READING RAINBOW SELECTION

Big & Little Book Library

Rockabye Crocodile
by Jose Aruego and Ariane Dewey

Putting on a Play
by Caroline Feller Bauer
Illustrations by Cyd Moore
* CHRISTOPHER AWARD AUTHOR

We Are Best Friends
by Aliki
* CHILDREN'S CHOICE AUTHOR

Fables from Around the World
retold by Lily Toy Hong, Carmen Tafolla, Tom Paxton, Joseph Bruchac, and Nancy Ross Ryan

Wings: A Tale of Two Chickens
by James Marshall
* CHILDREN'S CHOICE AUTHOR
* PARENTS' CHOICE AUTHOR
* ALA NOTABLE BOOK AUTHOR

Is There Life in Outer Space?
by Franklyn M. Branley
Illustrations by Don Madden
* READING RAINBOW BOOK

The Big Blank Piece of Paper

ARTISTS AT WORK

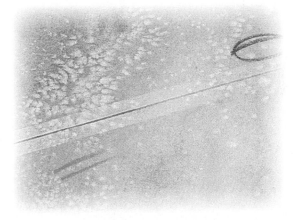

About the Cover Artist
Susan Melrath lives near Baltimore, Maryland, with her
husband, Brian Landgren. Her studio is in their home
in the country where she paints and is kept company by
Oz, Maggie, Rosco, and Coco—four furry friends.

ISBN 0-673-81131-X

1997
Scott, Foresman and Company, Glenview, Illinois
All Rights Reserved.
Printed in the United States of America.

Acknowledgments appear on page 128.

345678910DQ0100999897

The Big Blank Piece of Paper

ARTISTS AT WORK

ScottForesman

CONTENTS

Artists of Many Arts

Playtime

Genre Study

Meet Arnold Lobel

Author Study

I've Got It!

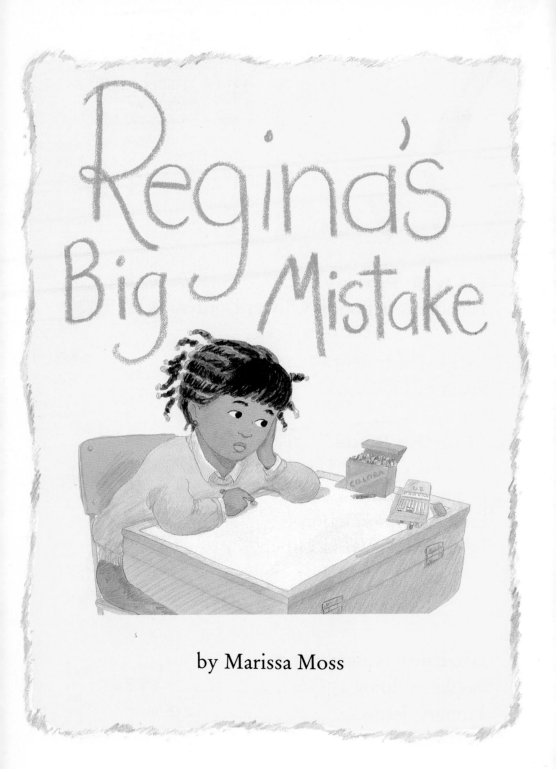

Regina's Big Mistake

by Marissa Moss

Everyone in Mrs. Li's class got a piece of paper. Everyone was supposed to draw a jungle or a rain forest. That meant Regina, too.

Regina stared at the big, blank piece of paper in front of her. Her fingers froze on her crayon. Where should she begin?

Stuart had already drawn two trees thick with leaves. Nathalie was concentrating on a fierce lion.

All around Regina jungles sprouted up. But her paper stayed blank.

"What are you making," joked Joshua, "an invisible jungle? Ha!"

Regina turned red. She hunched over her paper and lightly touched it with the tip of her crayon. She started to draw a jungle flower. She drew one petal, then another. But the second petal was bigger than the first one.

Regina groaned. A mistake! She tried to erase the second petal, but crayon doesn't erase, and she tore the paper instead. She crumpled it up quickly, before anyone could see her ugly mistake.

"What happened to your drawing?" asked Mrs. Li.

"I made a mistake," Regina mumbled.

"Well, try to draw around it next time," said Mrs. Li. "You're wasting paper."

Regina smoothed her new piece of paper. Anything was possible as long as it was empty. But somehow her hand could never draw what she saw in her head.

Stuart's jungle was almost finished now, full of strange, ripe fruits and colorful birds. Nathalie's lion stalked an antelope. Regina wanted to cry. She could never draw anything so beautiful.

"Almost done?" asked Mrs. Li. "Ten more minutes."

Regina picked up a brown crayon. She had to draw something. Carefully, she started to draw a tree like Stuart's.

"Hey, don't copy me!" he growled.

"I'm not," said Regina, and she quickly drew three big branches on her tree. But those heavy branches made her tree look funny.

Regina bit her lip. Was this another mistake? Could she draw around it, like Mrs. Li said? She looked again at the jungles growing around her.

"It's not a mistake. I can fix it," muttered Regina. She started to draw a lion under the tree.

"Copycat!" said Nathalie with a sneer.

"I am not!" Regina gulped. "My lion is different from yours." And she quickly drew a tongue hanging out of the lion's mouth.

"My lion's thirsty," said Regina. "He needs water." So she drew a lake, then a frog, some fish, and a duck to go in the lake, and some flowers alongside it. The jungle grew and grew until it filled the paper.

Regina smiled. All her jungle needed now was a sun. She carefully drew a yellow circle, but the crayon wobbled and the circle had a dent in it.

"I've ruined it!" she cried. "Just when it was getting good!"

"No more paper," warned Mrs. Li. "You'll have to make the best of it."

"Yeah," joked Joshua, "just pretend it's a very lumpy banana."

Regina looked hard at the wobbly circle. It wasn't a sun. But it wasn't a lumpy banana, either. Suddenly she recognized what it was. It was a moon! She drew a face in her moon and surrounded it with stars and comets and a purple-black sky.

"Wow!" said Stuart. "What a great idea! A jungle at night!"

"I wish I'd thought of that," said Nathalie.

Mrs. Li tacked all the pictures up on the wall.

"Good work, Regina," she said, smiling. "I love your moon."

The jungles glowed
with their bright colors. Each
one was different. Each one was
beautiful. And even with all her mistakes,
Regina thought hers was perfect.

Regina

Thinking About It

1. A night in the jungle! Where did Regina get her ideas for her drawing? Where do you get your ideas for your drawings?

2. A lumpy banana sun! Be Regina and tell what you learned from your mistake.

3. If Regina had to write a story to go with her picture, what would it be? Tell why you think so.

Another Book About Art

The Art Lesson, by Tomie dePaola, tells about a young artist whose teacher won't let him use his brand-new crayons.

A Good Play

We built a ship upon the stairs
All made of the back-bedroom chairs,
And filled it full of sofa pillows
To go a-sailing on the billows.

We took a saw and several nails,
And water in the nursery pails;
And Tom said, "Let us also take
An apple and a slice of cake";
Which was enough for Tom and me
To go a-sailing on, till tea.

We sailed along for days and days
And had the very best of plays;
But Tom fell out and hurt his knee,
So there was no one left but me.

—*Robert Louis Stevenson*

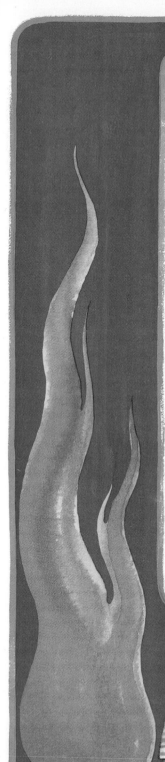

Celebration

I shall dance tonight.
When the dusk comes crawling,
There will be dancing
   and feasting.
I shall dance with the others
   in circles,
      in leaps,
         in stomps.
Laughter and talk
   will weave into the night,
Among the fires
   of my people.
Games will be played
And I shall be
   a part of it.

—*Alonzo Lopez*

Busy Summer

Bees
make wax and honey,

Spiders,
webs of silk.

Wasps
make paper houses.

Cows
make cream and milk.

Dandelions
make pollen
for the bees to take.

Wish that I
had something
I knew how to make.

—Aileen Fisher

The Secret Place

It was my secret place—
    down at the foot
    of my bed—
    under the covers.

It was very white.

I went there
    with a book, a flashlight,
    and the special pencil
    that my grandfather gave me.

To read—
    and to draw pictures
    on all that white.

It was my secret place
    for about a week—

Until my mother came
    to change the sheets.

       —*Tomie dePaola*

Painting Poetry

by Tomie dePaola

Tomie

The poems you read are from my book of poems. I read many different poems and picked out my favorites to illustrate for the book.

The nice thing about illustrating poetry is that every page is something brand-new. With most books, I have to do many pictures for the same story. But with my book of poems, I could paint different characters and use different colors on each page. Illustrating the poems was like doing many little paintings. I had fun!

You read one poem that I wrote myself, "The Secret Place." It's about me. I knew I was going to be an artist when I was four years old.

I really did draw on my sheets—I drew on anything white! Back then, my mother wasn't too pleased. But now that I am a well-known artist, she is sorry that she washed those sheets!

I like poetry because it tells about the ideas and feelings people have deep inside. What do you like about poetry? If you enjoyed reading these poems, you might like the other poems in my book, *Tomie dePaola's Book of Poems.*

TOTEM POLE BOY

From *U*S* Kids Magazine*

by Deborah H. DeFord

David Boxley and his father walk
through the woods. They are looking for
the perfect tree. It must be a cedar tree.
It must be tall and straight. It should not
have many branches.

David and his father are Tsimshian
Indians. David's father is also an artist. He
carves wood. He and David are looking for
a tree to carve into a totem pole. When the
totem pole is finished, it will tell the story
of their Indian tribe.

David's father cuts down the tree
they find. He cuts off all the branches.

Then David's father
tells David that he
sees pictures hidden
in the wood of the
tree. He carves the
wood until the pictures
appear.

What pictures does David's father see? He sees pictures from the Tsimshian tribe's history. The pictures may be people of the tribe. Or they may be animals.

David is proud to be a member of his tribe. And he's proud to be the son of the woodcarver who tells the story of his tribe on a tall cedar tree.

THINKING ABOUT IT

1 David is proud to be a totem pole boy. When are you proud like David? What have you made with someone that makes you proud?

2 Be David. David, you are learning more than woodcarving from your father. What else are you learning?

3 If you made a totem pole, what would you have it show? Why?

Another Book About David
You can see how David and his father's totem pole turns out in *Totem Pole* by Diane Hoyt-Goldsmith.

TOTEM POLE

BY DIANE HOYT-GOLDSMITH
PHOTOGRAPHS BY LAWRENCE MIGDALE

EMMA'S DRAGON HUNT

Written and illustrated by Catherine Stock

Emma was excited. Her Grandfather Wong from China was coming to live with them.

But when her grandfather arrived, he didn't look happy.

"The house is right on top of the hill and the roof is too flat," he grumbled. "I can't live here."

Emma looked at her grandfather, puzzled. "Why not, Grandfather?" she asked.

Grandfather Wong turned around and looked at her. "Because there are sure to be dragons living in the hill under the house. They will dance on the flat roof and keep me awake all night," he said.

That night Emma couldn't sleep.

Mother was cross with Grandfather Wong the next morning. "How can Emma concentrate on her lessons when she hasn't slept because of this dragon nonsense?"

"It's not nonsense," Grandfather Wong answered quietly.

That night when Grandfather Wong came in to say good night, Emma had all her stuffed animals with her in bed.

"You mustn't be afraid of the dragons," he said. "Our Chinese dragons are good dragons."

"But what do they look like?" Emma asked nervously.

Grandfather took a deep breath. "A Chinese dragon has the head of a camel, the neck of a snake, the horns of a stag, the eyes of a demon, the ears of a bull, the belly of a clam, the pads of a tiger, the tail of a lizard, the wings and claws of an eagle, the scales of a carp, and the whiskers of Wang Fu, the philosopher."

"Sounds scary to me," whispered Emma.

"No, no. Not at all," Grandfather assured her. "Tomorrow we'll hunt for one. You'll see."

The next morning Emma was so excited that she could hardly wait for Grandfather Wong to finish his second cup of tea.

"Well, now," he said at last. "Dragons like wet and marshy places."

So Emma took Grandfather to see the stream next to the house. She didn't find a dragon, but she did find a ball.

"Dragons love to play ball," said Grandfather Wong. "There must be one close by."

They walked up into the hills. No
dragons!

"When it's hot like this, they go
underground where it's cooler. These
mountains hold many dragon tunnels,"
explained Grandfather.

Suddenly the earth began to tremble and quake. Emma and her grandfather tumbled down in a heap.

"Was that a dragon?" asked Emma.

Grandfather Wong nodded. "We'll come back tomorrow."

The next day was unusually hot.
Emma and Grandfather Wong set off again,
hand in hand.

"I made this little paper dragon to put in
the sun," he said. "If it gets hot enough,
a real dragon sleeping under the hill will
wake up."

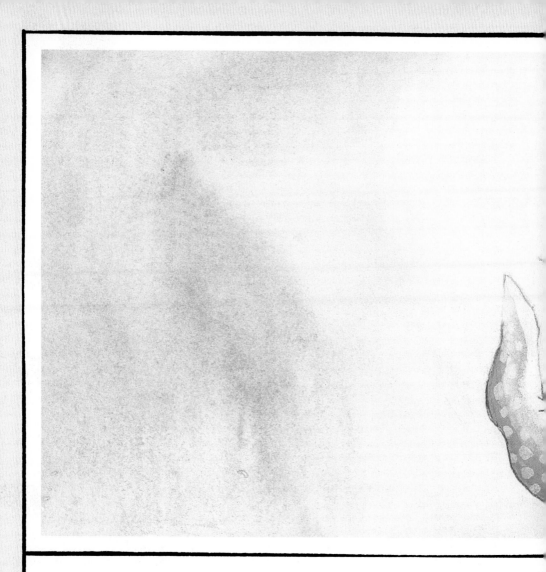

Everything began to grow dark.
Grandfather and Emma looked up at
the sky. The sun was slowly disappearing!

"Oh, dear," muttered Grandfather. "The dragon is so angry with the sun for waking him that he is trying to swallow it. But don't worry. The sun is so hot that he'll soon spit it out."

And he did. The sun came out again,
but billowy clouds of steam had gathered in
the sky. They began to darken. Emma and her
grandfather ran for cover as thunder boomed
across the sky.

"The dragon is still angry," Grandfather shouted above the noise. "He and his friends are knocking the clouds together. Boom! Boom! Luckily, their sharp claws rip open the clouds and let out all the rain."

It rained and it rained and it rained.

On Monday morning when Emma was getting ready for school, it was still raining.

"I'll ask Shom the Broom's daughter to sweep away those stormy dragons," Grandfather whispered to Emma. "She's a beautiful distant star."

"Where will she sweep them?" asked Emma.

"She sweeps them into the sea with all the clouds," Grandfather told her.

"Oh." Emma looked at a button on her raincoat.

"Dragons hunt for pearls in the sea. Their eyes are so sharp that fishermen paint dragon eyes on their boats to help them find fish," said Grandfather.

"I hope they come back," Emma said softly.

When Emma got home from school,
a brisk wind had swept all the clouds away.
Her grandfather had a surprise for her, a
beautiful dragon kite.

"It's to let the dragons know that we are their friends," he said.

At dinner everyone was talking about the things that had happened since Grandfather had arrived. There had been an earthquake, a heat wave, a solar eclipse, and a terrible thunderstorm followed by a beautiful rainbow.

Grandfather and Emma smiled, but they didn't say anything.

Grandfather Wong let Emma hang the kite in her room that night. She lay in bed and, just as she was falling asleep, she was sure that she could hear the pattering of dancing dragons on the roof.

THINKING ABOUT IT

1. Dragon nonsense! Or *is* it nonsense? Do dragons seem like nonsense to you? Tell Emma what she needs to know about this story.

2. Dragons are everywhere! How do Emma's feelings about the dragons change throughout the story? How do you know?

3. Do dragons really cause earthquakes? How might Grandfather Wong explain snow or fog? Why would he explain it that way?

Another Book About Dragons

Meet a holiday dragon in *Chinese New Year,* written by Tricia Brown and photographed by Fran Ortiz.

GIANTS

by *Syd Hoff*

Characters: Classroom of children.
The teacher.

Setting: A classroom.

(Two children are standing on tiptoes. They make themselves look big by sticking out their chests, clenching their fists, and stretching out their arms. They talk in deep, loud voices.)

First Child: We're giants.

Second Child: Great big giants.

First Child: We can see over trees and mountains.

Second Child: And tall buildings.

(Three more children enter and listen. They look like normal children.)

First Child: Hooray for us giants.

Second Child: We're not afraid of anybody.

Together: Hooray! Hooray!

Third Child: May we be giants, too?

Fourth Child: May we?

Fifth Child: *Please?*

First Child: No, you're too small.

Second Child: You're too little.

First Child: To be a giant, you must be big.

Second Child: Big like us.

Third Child: Then we'll get big.

Fourth Child: Big like you.

Fifth Child: Just you watch and see.

(The new children make themselves bigger by imitating the first two children. They stand on their tiptoes and throw out their chests. They clench their fists and stick out their arms. They start talking in deep, loud voices.)

Third Child: There! Now we're big.

Fourth Child: Big like you.

Fifth Child: Now we're giants too.

First Child: Hooray for us giants.

Second Child: We're not afraid of anybody.

All: *Hooray! Hooray!*

(Footsteps are heard in the distance, getting louder and louder.)

Second Child: Shhhhhh! What's that?

Second Child: It sounds like footsteps.

Third Child: Coming closer and closer.

Fourth Child: Maybe it's a giant.

Fifth Child: A *real* giant!

First Child: Ooh! What should we do?

Second Child: Let's make a run for it.

Third Child: Let's run before the giant sees us.

Fourth Child: Before it's too late.

Fifth Child: Before he eats us up!

First Child: No, let's stay right here. Maybe the giant will think we're real giants too, and leave us alone.

Second Child: Shhhhhh! Here's the giant now.

(Enter the teacher.)

Giant: *(Sniffing.)* Fee, fie, fo, fum! Yummy, yum, yum! I smell little children I can eat for my supper.

First Child: We're not children, Giant.

Second Child: We're not children at all.

Third Child: We're giants.

Fourth Child: Giants like you.

Fifth Child: Just like you.

Giant: Hmmmm . . . so I see. You're much too big to be children. Oh, well, if I can't eat my supper, I may as well go to sleep. That's what I always do on an empty stomach.

(The giant falls asleep. He puts his face in his hands and closes his eyes.)

First Child: The giant is asleep.

Third Child: Let's run away now.

Fourth Child: Run for our lives.

Fifth Child: Run while we can.

First Child: No, no! The giant might awaken and catch us. I have a better idea. Listen.

(He covers his mouth as if whispering, and they lean forward as if to listen.)

Second Child: That's a good idea.

Third Child: A great idea.

Fourth Child: Let's do it, quickly.

Fifth Child: Before he awakens.

(The children try to look smaller by shrinking down. They hunch their bodies. They form a circle around the giant. They talk in high voices.)

First Child: *(Whispering.)* You know what to say. Now!

All: Wake up, giant! Wake up! Look! Look! Look at us!

Giant: *(Opening eyes.)* Wh-what is it?

First Child: A terrible thing has happened to us.

Second Child: A giant shrinker came along and put a spell on us.

Giant: A giant shrinker?

Third Child: Yes, he made us small.

Fifth Child: But we're *still giants.*

Giant: (*Scratching his head.*) Oh, what a terrible thing. Look at you! Why, you have shrunk to the size of children!

First Child: The giant shrinker didn't notice you because you were asleep.

Second Child: But he may come back.

Third Child: You'd better get away fast.

Fourth Child: Before he comes back.

Fifth Child: Before he makes you shrink, too.

Giant: Oh, yes! Yes! I'd better get away fast, before the giant shrinker returns. Thanks, thanks, all you giants, for saving me.

(*He hurries off. The children become normal in size and talk in normal voices.*)

All: Hooray! Hooray! It worked! It worked! The giant is gone! We're saved! We're saved!

First Child: It was fun being giants.

Second Child: But let's not be giants anymore.

Third Child: Let's be ourselves.

Fifth Child: Just the way we are.

First Child: I'm so hungry I could eat a giant.

Second Child: A giant ice cream cone.

Third Child: Or a giant hot dog.

Fourth Child: Or a giant hamburger.

Fifth Child: Hooray for giants!

First Child: Hooray for us!

All: Hooray! Hooray!

The Chicken
and
The Egg

by Judith Martin

cast

Chickens   Eggs

costumes

- paper-cone noses
- eyeglasses
- tails made of newspaper strips

- white turtleneck sweaters

*(All the **Eggs** are on one side of the stage. All the **Chickens** are on the other side of the stage. **First Egg** and **First Chicken** rush to center of stage.)*

First Egg: I was here first.

First Chicken: I was here first.

First Egg: I was here first.

First Chicken: I was here first.

First Egg: I was here first.

First Egg and First Chicken: *(Sing)*
    All my life I've been in doubt.
    Won't you please help me out?
    Which came first?
    The chicken or the egg,
    Or the egg or the chicken
    Or the chicken or the egg?

(First Egg and First Chicken rejoin their friends. There is a hubbub of talk in each group. Second Chicken and Second Egg rush to center of stage.)

Second Egg: I was here first.

Second Chicken: I was here first.

Second Egg: I beg your pardon.

Second Chicken: I beg your pardon.

Second Egg and Second Chicken: *(Sing)*
All my life I've been in doubt.
Won't you please help me out?

All: Which came first?
The chicken or the egg,
Or the egg or the chicken
Or the chicken or the egg?

(All Chickens and all Eggs rush excitedly around the stage. Each Chicken finds an Egg and in pairs they argue.)

Third Chicken: How can there be any doubt?
If you didn't have a chicken,
An egg couldn't come out!

Fourth Chicken: Where do you think you would be? Without me you wouldn't be.

Fifth Chicken: Anybody can see that I came first. There's more to me than there is to you. I have a beak. I have wings and feathers. You're nothing but a blank empty shape.

Third Egg: Who needs all those foolish feathers, anyway? I'll have you know I'm the basic original shape. It's simple, it's beautiful, and it works.

First Chicken: What are you talking about? I know much more than you because I'm older than you. I've been an egg; you've never been a chicken.

First Egg: Which proves my point. You've been an egg, which shows you that an egg came first.

Second Egg: Eggsactly.

Second Chicken: But, but, but, but you had to come from something, like perhaps maybe a chicken.

All Chickens: Cluck. Cluck.

Fourth Egg: Well, it certainly gives you something to think about.

All: *(Sing and dance)*
    All my life I've been in doubt.
    Won't you please help me out?
    Which came first?
    The chicken or the egg,
    Or the egg or the chicken
    Or the chicken or the egg?

Fourth Egg: I don't care what those birdbrains say,
    I feel first.

Third Egg: I feel first too; way down deep in my yolk,
    I feel first.

First Chicken: Listen, don't listen to those brainless
    creatures.

Second Chicken: I don't take them seriously. They're
    cracked.

Eggs: I was here first.

Chickens: I was here first.

All: All my life I've been in doubt.
    Won't you please help me out?
    Which came first?
    The chicken or the egg,
    Or the egg or the chicken
    Or the chicken or the egg?

    (Entire cast exits quarreling and cackling.)

Thinking About It

1. Do you want to be a giant or a chicken? Choose your part and then get ready. Show three ways you'll get ready for your part.

2. People will come to see these two plays. List things you need to do to put on the plays. Do this before the people get there!

3. To put on a play, you must have a story. Find or make up two more stories that would be good plays. Explain why they would be good plays.

The Story

by Arnold Lobel

One day in summer Frog was not feeling well.

Toad said, "Frog, you are looking quite green."

"But I always look green," said Frog.

"I am a frog."

"Today you look very green even for a frog," said Toad. "Get into my bed and rest."

Toad made Frog a cup of hot tea.

Frog drank the tea, and then he said, "Tell me a story while I am resting."

"All right," said Toad. "Let me think of a story to tell you."

Toad thought and thought. But he could not think of a story to tell Frog.

"I will go out on the front porch and walk up and down," said Toad. "Perhaps that will help me to think of a story."

Toad walked up and down on the porch for a long time. But he could not think of a story to tell Frog.

Then Toad went into the house and stood on his head.

"Why are you standing on your head?" asked Frog.

"I hope that if I stand on my head, it will help me to think of a story," said Toad.

Toad stood on his head for a long time. But he could not think of a story to tell Frog.

Then Toad poured a glass of water over his head.

"Why are you pouring water over your head?" asked Frog.

"I hope that if I pour water over my head, it will help me to think of a story," said Toad.

Toad poured many glasses of water over his head. But he could not think of a story to tell Frog.

Then Toad began to
bang his head against
the wall.

"Why are you
banging your head
against the wall?"
asked Frog.

"I hope that if I bang
my head against the wall
hard enough, it will help
me to think of a story,"
said Toad.

"I am feeling much
better now, Toad," said
Frog. "I do not think I
need a story anymore."

"Then you get out of bed and let me get into it," said Toad, "because now I feel terrible."

Frog said, "Would you like me to tell you a story, Toad?"

"Yes," said Toad, "if you know one."

"Once upon a time," said Frog, "there were two good friends, a frog and a toad. The frog was not feeling well. He asked his friend the toad to tell him a story.

"The toad could not think of a story. He walked up and down on the porch, but he could not think of a story. He stood on his head, but he could not think of a story. He poured water over his head, but he could not think of a story. He banged his head against the wall, but he still could not think of a story.

"Then the toad did not feel so well, and the frog was feeling better. So the toad went to bed and the frog got up and told him a story. The end. How was that, Toad?" said Frog.

But Toad did not answer. He had fallen asleep.

PIGERICKS

— by Arnold Lobel —

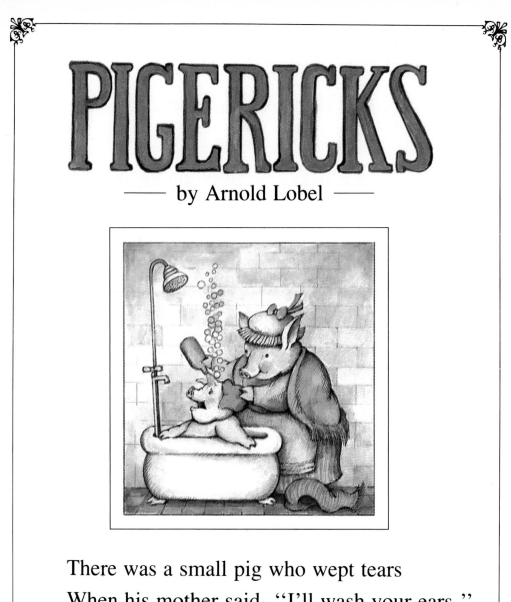

There was a small pig who wept tears
When his mother said, "I'll wash your ears."
As she poured on the soap,
He cried, "Oh, how I hope
This won't happen again for ten years!"

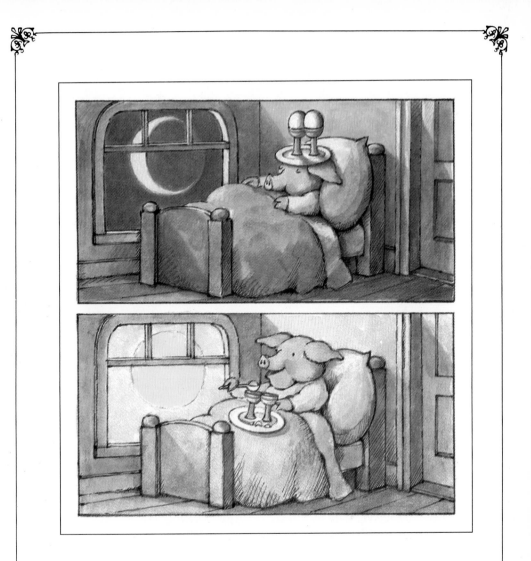

There was a young pig who, in bed,
Nightly slumbered with eggs on his head.
When the sun at its rise
Made him open his eyes,
He enjoyed a quick breakfast in bed.

There was a warm pig from Key West.
Of sandcastles, his was the best.
But as soon as he built it,
A wave came to tilt it,
Which dampened that pig from Key West.

There was an old pig with a pen
Who wrote stories and verse now and then.
To enhance these creations,
He drew illustrations
With brushes, some paints and his pen.

ARNOLD LOBEL

A Man Who Loved Stories

by George Shannon

Arnold Lobel has been one of my favorite writers for many years. And the story of Arnold Lobel himself is one of my favorite stories. When I wrote a book about him, I visited him at home to learn more about his life.

When Arnold was a child, his talent for making stories helped him through a hard time. Because of a serious illness, Arnold missed every day of the second grade and couldn't play with his friends. When he finally went back to school, not many children remembered him. They laughed at him too. He still had to learn many things they could already do.

But there was one thing Arnold *could* do
that most other children could not. He could tell
his class stories and draw illustrations on the big
chalkboard. The children liked his stories so
much that Arnold made new friends.

When Arnold grew up, he began making books for children. He loved to tell stories about animals who acted like people. Since everyone can pretend to be an animal, Arnold knew everyone could pretend to be in his books.

One of Arnold's favorite writers and artists was Edward Lear, who wrote nonsense poems called "limericks." Arnold wanted to write poems like that, but he didn't want to copy. So Arnold called his limericks "pigericks" and drew pigs in all his pictures. One pig even looked like him!

Many of Arnold's ideas for stories came from his own life. When Arnold's children were small, they had frogs and toads for pets. Now Frog and Toad are the best-known characters Arnold created.

Arnold Lobel died in 1987, but his books are still read by people around the world. Whenever we read his stories and poems, we are sharing some of the things he liked best— nonsense, laughter, and friends who love good stories.

THINKING ABOUT IT

1. Toad stood on his head to get an idea for a story, but it didn't work! How do you get ideas for stories?

2. Ha! Ha! Ha! What do you think makes Arnold Lobel's stories and poems funny? Explain.

3. Arnold Lobel had fun writing limericks about pigs. What animal would you enjoy writing a limerick about? Why? What would you call your limerick?

More Stories About Frog and Toad

Frog and Toad have more adventures in *Frog and Toad Are Friends.*

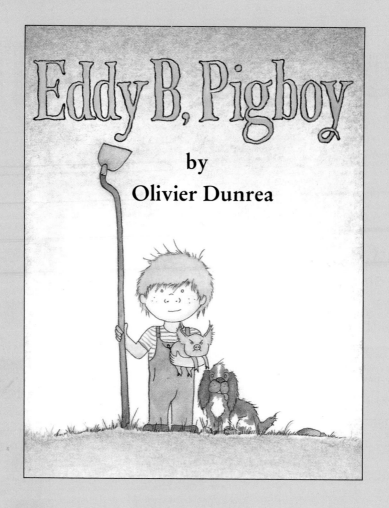

Eddy B, Pigboy

by
Olivier Dunrea

My name is Eddy B.

I live on a farm.

I have a Pa, a Ma, two sisters, and a little brother.

And a dog named Daisy D.

I work on my Pa's farm as a pigboy.

When a mama pig wanders off with her babies, my job is to find them because wild animals can hurt the piglets.

So, I go out and hunt for the mama pig. It's up to me to get her and her babies home safe.

When I find the mama pig and the
piglets, I sneak up real quiet, and quick
as lightning grab one of the piglets and
hold on to it real tight.

Right away the little porker lets out the
loudest squeal you've ever heard.
That's when I start running back to the
farm as fast as I can.

When the mama pig hears her baby
squealing like that, she wants to get
whoever is hurting it. That's why she
comes after me and that's why I run.

I head right for the pigsty running for all
I'm worth. Because if mama pig catches
me she can be awful mean and bite hard.
And mama pigs run fast.

As soon as I get to the pigsty I throw the little squealer in and, quick as I can, I jump onto the fence.

When I was little and not so fast, a mama pig tore out the seat of my pants as I was trying to climb the fence. I run real fast now.

Mama pig runs right into the sty to find
her baby and all the other little ones
follow right behind her as fast as they
can. Pa shuts the gate real quick.

Mama pig makes sure her baby is okay.

Then she lies down to nurse all of them.

My job is done.

For running as a pigboy Pa gives me a quarter. And with that quarter I buy the biggest ice cream soda in the world.

Then Daisy D and I go fishing.

And that's what a pigboy does.

Thinking About It

1. Now it is mama pig's turn to tell what Eddy B does. Let's hear her story.

2. What do you like about the way Eddy B catches pigs? What don't you like about it? Explain how *you* would get the pigs.

3. Eddy B's little brother has gotten lost. How will Eddy B find him? Why do you think so?

Another Book by Olivier Dunrea

A treasure map! In *Fergus and Bridey*, Fergus and his dog set off in their boat to find a buried treasure.

Pete Pats Pigs
By Dr. Seuss

Pete Briggs pats pigs.

Briggs pats pink pigs.

Briggs pats big pigs.

(Don't ask me why. It doesn't matter.)

Pete Briggs is a pink pig, big pig patter.

Pete Briggs pats his big pink pigs all day.

(Don't ask me why. I cannot say.)

Then Pete puts his patted pigs away

in his Pete Briggs' Pink Pigs Big Pigs Pigpen.

FOR
THE
Birds

by the Earth Works Group

Splash! Ruffle! Splash! Have you ever watched a bird take a bath? It dips in, fluffs itself up, shakes all over, flaps its wings and dips and flaps some more. . . . And it looks like it's having the greatest time. Probably it is!

That's why there are so many birds in yards with birdbaths. Setting up a bath or feeder is a great way to bring birds into your yard. And when you do, you not only get to enjoy the birds, you also get to help the Earth.

Take a Guess . . .

What is a hummingbird's favorite food?
A) Hot oatmeal B) Sweet syrup C) Corn-on-the-cob

Did You Know

- Birds are always hungry! They use up so much energy that they need to eat all the time.
- Sometimes birds eat $\frac{4}{5}$ of their own weight in one day!
- What does that mean? Let's say you weigh 100 pounds. If you were a bird, you would have to eat 80 pounds of food between the time you woke up in the morning and the time you went to sleep at night! You can't do it! But birds can.
- Birds need water to drink (especially in summer) and to keep clean. They can have anywhere from 940 to 25,000 feathers, so they've got a lot of washing to do!

Answer: B. Little hummingbirds love sweet syrup or water with a bit of sugar.

113

What You Can Do

• Make a birdfeeder for peanuts! Take a bunch of unsalted peanuts still in their shells, and tie them on a piece of yarn or string. Hang the string from a branch; birds will find it.

• Another nutty idea: Spread peanut butter all over a pine cone. Be sure to fill up all the little spaces. Then hang the pine cone outside. Lots of birds like peanut butter.

• Hang some orange peels from trees— a great bird snack!

Make a Birdbath

• Find a big ceramic or plastic saucer like the kind under potted plants. (Don't use metal—it will get too hot in the summer and freeze in the winter.) It should have some kind of edge around it for birds to rest on.

• Birds don't need the water to be too deep—about two inches is perfect. Keep the bath filled with water.

• If there are cats in the neighborhood, you might need to put the birdbath up high or hang it from a tree.

PULLING THE THEME
together

Creativity

1. Birds need you. What have you found out that will make you a better friend of birds?

2. Drawings! Plays! Poems! Stories! Totem poles! These are all ways to be creative. How are they alike? How are they different? Use examples from the book to help you explain.

3. It's Emma's birthday, and she's having a party. But Regina, Toad, and Eddy don't have any money. What will each one bring? Why do you think so?

BOOKS to ENJOY

Owl at Home
Written and illustrated by Arnold Lobel

Owl is afraid of two bumps at the foot of his bed. They move whenever his feet move. Owl thinks he will never get to sleep!

Pigs Aplenty, Pigs Galore!
Written and illustrated by David McPhail

The author has drawn himself into this story about one night when he discovers a pile of pigs in his kitchen — oh, oh!

Magic Secrets
by Rose Wyler and Gerald Adams

Step right up! Learn easy magic tricks to show your best friends. This book will tell you how.

Cherries and Cherry Pits

Written and illustrated by Vera B. Williams

Bidemmi makes up stories about the people she draws. Before long, she draws herself into a story too.

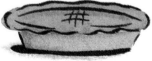

Liang and the Magic Paintbrush

Written and illustrated by Demi
Liang loves to paint with his magic paintbrush. Everything he paints comes to life! But the wicked emperor wants this magic brush for himself.

Build It with Boxes

by Joan Irvine
Illustrations by Linda Hendry

You can recycle to make anything you want. Will it be a clubhouse or a sports car? Perhaps a moon suit? Read tips and then decide.

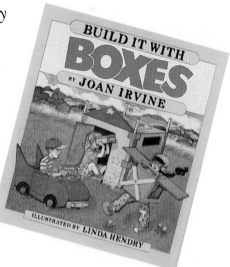

LITERARY TERMS

Fiction

Fiction is a kind of story that comes from an author's imagination. Marissa Moss made up the story *Regina's Big Mistake*, so that story is fiction.

Informational Article

An **informational article** is nonfiction writing that tells you about something that has really happened. "Totem Pole Boy" tells how a boy and his father carve a totem pole.

TOTEM POLE BOY

by Deborah H. DeFord

David Boxley and his father walk through the woods. They are looking for the perfect tree. It must be a cedar tree. It must be tall and straight. It should not have many branches.

David and his father are Tsimshian Indians. David's father is also an artist. He carves wood. He and David are looking for a tree to carve into a totem pole. When the totem pole is finished, it will tell the story of their Indian tribe.

David's father cuts down the tree they find. He cuts off all the branches.

Limerick

A **limerick** is a funny poem that has five lines. The pigericks on pages 90–93 are really limericks.

Nonfiction

Nonfiction is a kind of writing that tells facts about real people or things. Nonfiction can also tell how to do something. "For the Birds" tells how you can make bird feeders.

Play

A **play** is a story that is written to be acted out. "The Chicken and the Egg" is a play.

Poetry

Poetry is writing that uses rhythm and words to make you think or feel about something in a special way. How do you feel after reading the poem "Celebration" on page 31?

Glossary

Words from your stories

billow

bang to make or cause to make a sudden, loud noise: *The baby was banging the pan with a spoon.* **banged, banging.**

billow a huge wave: *The ship tossed and turned on the billows.* **billows.**

build to make by putting things together: *It takes many people to build a bridge.* **built, building.**

built See **build.**

cast

carve to cut pictures or designs into. **carved, carving.**

cast all the actors in a play: *The cast bowed at the end of the play.* **casts.**

ceramic made of clay: *Caleb gave his aunt a ceramic bowl for her birthday.*

China a large country in Asia: *Wang Li's family comes from China.*

clench to close together tightly: *He shook his clenched fist at us.* **clenched, clenching.**

concentrate to pay close attention; to think hard about something: *The movie was confusing so I tried to concentrate as I watched.* **concentrated, concentrating.**

copycat a person who copies someone else's work or actions: *Joel is a copycat because he likes to do what others do.* **copycats.**

costume clothes that a person can put on to look like someone or something else: *Costumes are often worn in plays.* **costumes.**

costume

crawl **1.** to move slowly on hands and knees: *Babies crawl before they begin to walk.* **2.** to move slowly: *The heavy traffic crawled through the tunnel.* **crawled, crawling.**

crumple to crush together; wrinkle: *I crumpled the shopping list and threw it away.* **crumpled, crumpling.**

crawl

doubt being without belief; feeling uncertain: *His doubts about the team disappeared when they won.* **doubts.**

123

dragon

dragon in stories, a huge, fierce animal that was said to look like a lizard: *Dragons are supposed to breathe out fire and smoke.* **dragons.**

dusk the time just before dark: *The setting sun brought dusk to the forest.*

energy one's power to work or move or play: *My sister has so much energy she can't sit still.*

excited having very strong, happy feelings about something that you like: *I am excited about seeing the circus.*

giant

fluff to shake or puff out: *Harry fluffed up his pillow.* **fluffed, fluffing.**

giant 1. in stories, a person of very large size: *The giant in the story was friendly.* 2. huge: *We made a giant sandwich for lunch.* **giants.**

jungle

invisible not able to be seen: *Germs are invisible.*

jungle a kind of forest, with thick bushes, vines, and many trees: *Jungles are found in hot countries.* **jungles.**

124

member   someone who belongs to a group: *Our singing group has four members.* **members.**

metal   a hard, shiny material such as iron, gold, silver, or steel: *Metals can be melted or hammered into thin sheets.* **metals.**

mistake   something that is not right or done the way it ought to be: *I made a mistake in adding those numbers.* **mistakes.**

mistake

nonsense   words or ideas that don't make sense: *The talk about the haunted house in town was nonsense.*

normal   usual or common: *This is normal weather for this time of year.*

nurse   **1.** a person who takes care of sick people: *Many nurses work in hospitals.* **2.** when a mother gives her milk to a baby: *The mother cat nursed her kittens.* **nurses; nursed, nursing.**

piglet

pigboy   a worker on a farm who takes care of the pigs: *Sam worked as a pigboy on Mr. Harris's farm.* **pigboys.**

piglet   a baby pig: *The piglets squealed for their dinner.* **piglets.**

pour

sandcastle

saucer

pigsty a place where pigs are kept; pigpen: *She cleaned out the pigsty for her mother.* **pigsties.**

pollen a fine dust or powder given off by flowers: *The bees carried pollen from place to place.*

pour to cause to flow in a steady stream: *I poured milk on my cereal.* **poured, pouring.**

puzzle **1.** a game that you work out for fun: *Help me put the pieces of this puzzle together.* **2.** to make it hard for someone to understand something; to confuse: *Why he left so early puzzled us.* **puzzles; puzzled, puzzling.**

rain forest a very thick forest in a place where rain is heavy all year long: *A rain forest is a home for many plants and animals.* **rain forests.**

sandcastle a castle made of sand on a beach: *My little brother built a huge sandcastle.* **sandcastles.**

saucer a small, shallow dish: *Joe handed me a cup of tea on a saucer.* **saucers.**

126

shrink to become smaller; to make something smaller: *Hot water will shrink my wool socks.* **shrank, shrunk, shrinking.**

sneak to move in a sly or secret way: *My cat likes to sneak up on the dog.* **sneaked, sneaking.**

sprout to start growing: *The buds are sprouting on that blackberry bush.* **sprouted, sprouting.**

sprout

squeal to cry in a sharp, shrill way: *The pigs squealed when they saw the dog.* **squealed, squealing.**

sty See **pigsty.**

tilt to tip or cause to fall forward: *The queen tilted her head when she bowed.* **tilted, tilting.**

tribe a group of people who have the same language and ways of doing things: *Many tribes of Plains Indians were hunters.* **tribes.**

tilt

weep to cry; sob with tears falling: *I began to weep with joy when I won the spelling bee.* **wept, weeping.**

wept See **weep.**

weep

127

Acknowledgments

Text

Page 8: *Regina's Big Mistake* by Marissa Moss. Copyright © 1990 by Marissa Moss. Reprinted by permission of Houghton Mifflin Co.

Pages 30–33: Reprinted by permission of G. P. Putnam's Sons from *Tomie dePaola's Book of Poems*. Illustrations copyright © 1988 by Tomie dePaola.

Page 31: "Celebration" by Alonzo Lopez from *Whispering Wind* by Terry Allen, copyright © 1972 by the Institute of American Indian Arts. Used by permission of Doubleday, a division of Bantam Dell Publishing Group, Inc.

Page 32: "Busy Summer" by Aileen Fisher from *In the Woods, In the Meadow, In the Sky*. Copyright © 1965 by Aileen Fisher. Reprinted by permission of the author.

Page 33: "The Secret Place" by Tomie dePaola and illustrations by Tomie dePaola reprinted by permission of G. P. Putnam's Sons from *Tomie dePaola's Book of Poems,* poem and illustrations copyright © 1988 by Tomie dePaola.

Page 34: "Painting Poetry," by Tomie dePaola. Copyright © by Tomie dePaola, 1991. Illustrations by Tomie dePaola reprinted by permission of G. P. Putnam's Sons from *Tomie dePaola's Book of Poems,* copyright © 1988 by Tomie dePaola.

Page 36: Special reprint permission granted by *U*S*Kids* magazine, published by Field Publications. Copyright © 1990 by Field Publications. *U*S*Kids* is a federally registered trademark of Field Publications.

Page 40: *Emma's Dragon Hunt* written and illustrated by Catherine Stock. Copyright © 1984 by Catherine Stock. Reprinted by permission of William Morrow and Company, Inc. Publishers.

Page 66: "Giants" by Syd Hoff. Reprinted by permission of the author and the author's agents, Scott Meredith Literary Agency, Inc. 845 Third Avenue, New York, New York 10022.

Page 74: "The Chicken and the Egg" by Judith Martin. From *Everybody, Everybody* by the Paper Bag Players. Copyright © 1981 by the Paper Bag Players. Used by permission of Lodestar Books, an affiliate of Dutton Children's Books, a division of Penguin Books USA Inc.

Page 82: "The Story" from *Frog and Toad Are Friends* by Arnold Lobel. Copyright © 1970 by Arnold Lobel. Reprinted by permission of HarperCollins Publishers.

Page 90: "Pigericks" from *The Book of Pigericks: Pig Limericks* by Arnold Lobel.

Copyright © 1983 by Arnold Lobel. Reprinted by permission of HarperCollins Publishers.

Page 94: "Arnold Lobel: A Man Who Loved Stories," by George Shannon. Copyright © by George Shannon, 1991. Illustrations are from *The Book of Pigericks: Pig Limericks* by Arnold Lobel. Copyright © 1983 by Arnold Lobel. Reprinted by permission of HarperCollins Publishers.

Page 98: *Eddie B, Pigboy* by Olivier Dunrea. Copyright © 1983 by Olivier Dunrea. Used by permission of Dell Books, a division of Bantam Doubleday Dell Publishing Group, Inc.

Page 110: "Pete Pats Pigs" from *Oh Say Can You Say?* by Dr. Seuss. Copyright © 1979 by Theodor S. Geisel and Audrey S. Geisel. Reprinted by permission of Random House, Inc.

Page 112: Text from "For the Birds" from *50 Simple Things Kids Can Do to Save the Earth*. Copyright © 1990 by John Javna. The EarthWorks Group. Published by Andrews and McMeel. Reprinted by permission.

Artists

Illustrations owned and copyrighted by the illustrator.

Mary Lynn Blasutta, cover, 1–7, 117–128
Marissa Moss, 8–29
Tomie dePaola, 30–35
Catherine Stock, 40–65
Hudson Talbott, 66–73, 81
John Holm, 74–81
Arnold Lobel, 82–97
Olivier Dunrea, 98–109
Dr. Seuss (Theodor S. Geisel), 110–111
Etienne Delessert, 112–116

Photographs

Unless otherwise acknowledged, all photographs are the property of Scott Foresman.

Page 35: Courtesy of Tomie dePaola
Pages 36–39: Photos by Lawrence Migdale
Page 95: Courtesy of HarperCollins Publishers

Glossary

The contents of this glossary have been adapted from *My Second Picture Dictionary*, Copyright © 1990 Scott, Foresman and Company and *Beginning Dictionary*, Copyright © 1988 Scott, Foresman and Company.